The Soldiers Handbook
Of Vulgar, Crude and Offensive Rhymes

This book is available on amazon

Search: Squaddie Brand Publishing on amazon

Copyright Squaddie Brand Publishing (SH) 2024

All Rights Reserved

This is an original book of Rhymes
So should not have been heard many times
Packed with Rhymes galore
You shouldn't have heard these before

Thank you for buying this book from me
I hope you enjoy it with fun and glee
Although I always joke and fart
I really do thank you from my heart

Disclaimer: All names of soldiers and characters are fictional and completely made up anybody resembling the soldiers or characters or having the same name(s) is purely coincidental

Do not take offense, they are only jokes not to be taken seriously

First Day In The Army

There was a boy that wanted to go in the army
All his mates thought he was barmy
One day he got on the train
In the pouring rain
And all he had to eat was a soggy sarnie

The train arrived in a strange town
On the platform was an NCO With a scary frown
"Get on them buses!"
He shouted with cusses
The recruits underpants were now brown

Arriving at the camp gate
It wasn't too late
To do a runner
But on second thoughts
With an expired train ticket
That could be a real bummer!

When they debussed
The NCO's sussed
What a crock of shit they were
It really was hard
To tell a him from a her

Filled with dread
They were allocated a bed
Hospital corners
Were the orders
But nothing more was said

Kit was handed out with a shout
Whether you were short or stout
When fully kitted
None of it fitted
And everything was itchy without a doubt

Drill was learnt
And respect was earnt
Not knowing left from right
Could end in a fight
But they knew already you were burnt

Marching up and down
You felt like a clown
"Quick March!
You need more starch!
You would be smarter in a dressing gown!"

The food was crude
In the short interlude
Potatoes like rocks
That tasted like socks
The only answer was for the cooks to be sued

Bulling boots
And ironing suits
The life of a recruit couldn't be meaner
After washing doors and polishing floors
You felt more like a cleaner

After a very long day
You hit the hay
With lights out at eleven
You shut your eyes and it felt like were in heaven
With no time to dally
It's already 6 a.m
And it's time for Reveille

Reveille

Reveille is a balls ache
Make no mistake
Time to take your hands off your personal snake
With determined grit
You get out of your pit
And now you are awake

The Sprog

When you're a sprog
You're treated ten times worse
Than a third world dog
You run up hills
Just for thrills
Every minute is a hard slog

You are inspected in the mornings
Without any warnings
Then you are cleaning the bogs
In this man's army
You are the very smallest of cogs

There's no solutions
To cleaning the ablutions
You just have to put your arm down the pan
It might be absurd
To pull up a turd
But it's all part of being a man

Bulling boots and pressing shirts
It said nothing of this in the army adverts

The boy in the next bed seems a bit dumb
The boy the other side is crying for his mum

Your family back home are on holiday in Spain
While you're in the pissing rain stuck on Salisbury Plain

Back home your mates are ripping off birds knickers and blouses
While you are confined to barracks cleaning shit houses

The troop commander seems very posh
While the troop sergeant is always cross
And nobody seems to give a fuck
That the troop corporal thinks he is the boss!

There is no drink
But you feel pissed
Because on the ranges
You hit much less than is missed!

The ranges are fun
They give you a gun
This is a real thriller!
Then you think to yourself
I hope this twat next to me
Is not a phsychotic serial killer!

Just when you think you are free
They give you PT
Running for miles
Until you've got piles
The only thing worse is VD

You bull your boots
Then get dressed
Feeling slightly depressed
They prescribe a happy pill
What's that? I hear you ask
Lots and lots of drill!

But it's all over soon this masquerade
You soon find yourself on the passing out parade
Standing tall and proud
In front of the crowd
With legs apart
You let out a fart
Fuck me that was loud!

The Assault Course

The assault course was always so much fun
You had to do it after a ten mile run

Clambering over walls so high
You would often get poked in the fucking eye

Crawling through tunnels like sewage pipes
There was no time for any gripes

Jumping into the scramble net
You were already soaking wet

Swinging across boggy water on the rope swing
Butterflies in the stomach it would bring

There was always some twat that fell in
Which was considered a regimental sin
Covered in shit and boggy poo
Then you realised that twat was YOU!!!

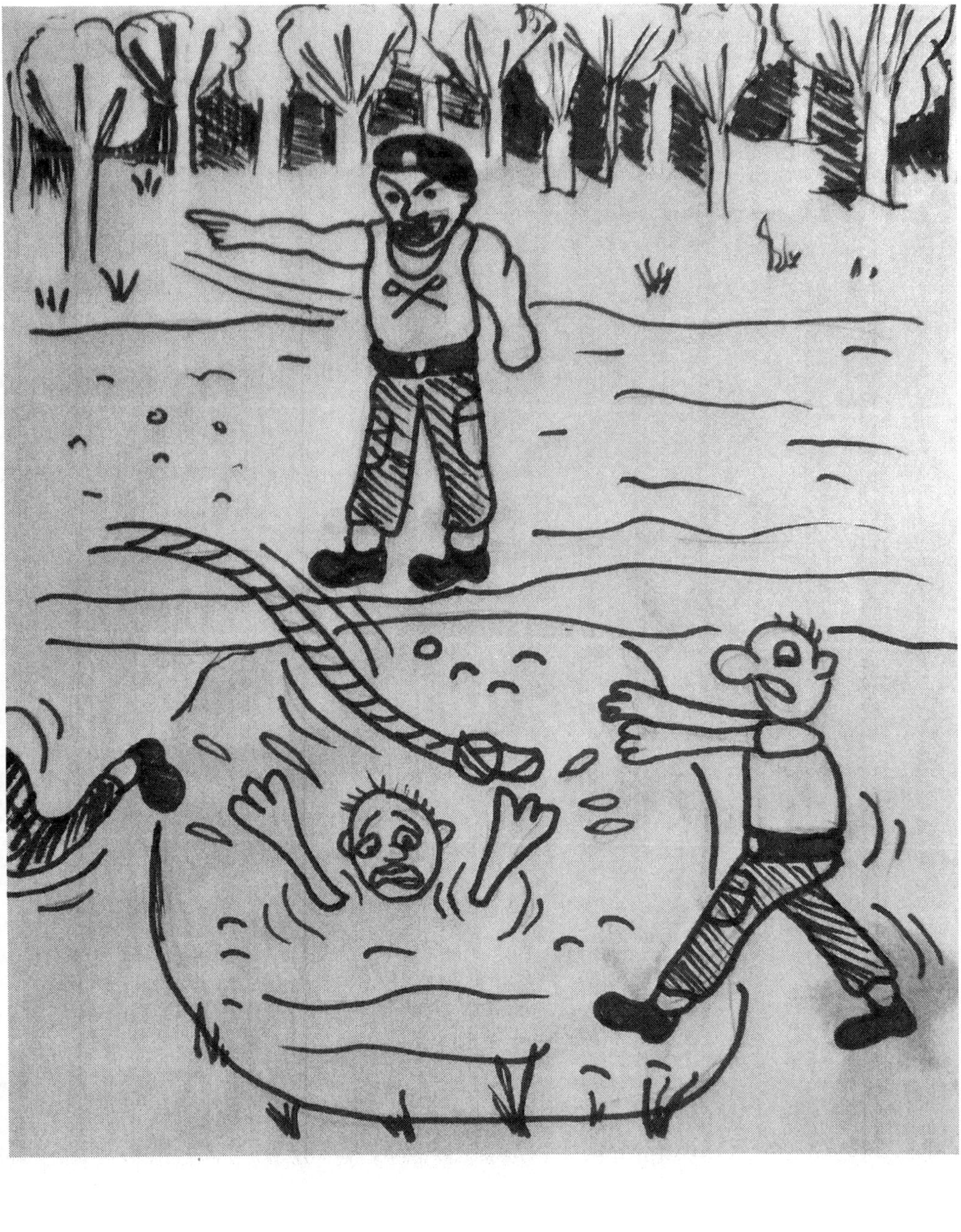

The Training Sergeant

The Training Sergeant is so much fun
On freezing mornings he insists on a run
Cleaning your weapon to perfection
You can be on a charge for calling it a gun!

The Troop Commander

The Troop Commander seems oh so posh
After swimming in a swamp
He insists on a wash
He dines very fine
While we all nosh
Then he says things like oh my gosh!

Army PTI's In Training

There once was a PTI
That would push you until you wanted to Die
"Have you been up the rope?" he said
Up and down I nodded my head
He wanted one more try
Because he knew it was a fucking lie

The PTI's in the army are such a thrill
They march you up and down Heartbreak Hill
Endless push ups and sit ups are such a treat
I wish I was back in Civvy Street

When's this nightmare going to end?
It's sending me around the fucking bend
After running so many miles
Chasing a four tonner truck
The only thing I can do now is puke up
So I run like fuck to the nearest shitter
When I re emerge I know I'm much fitter

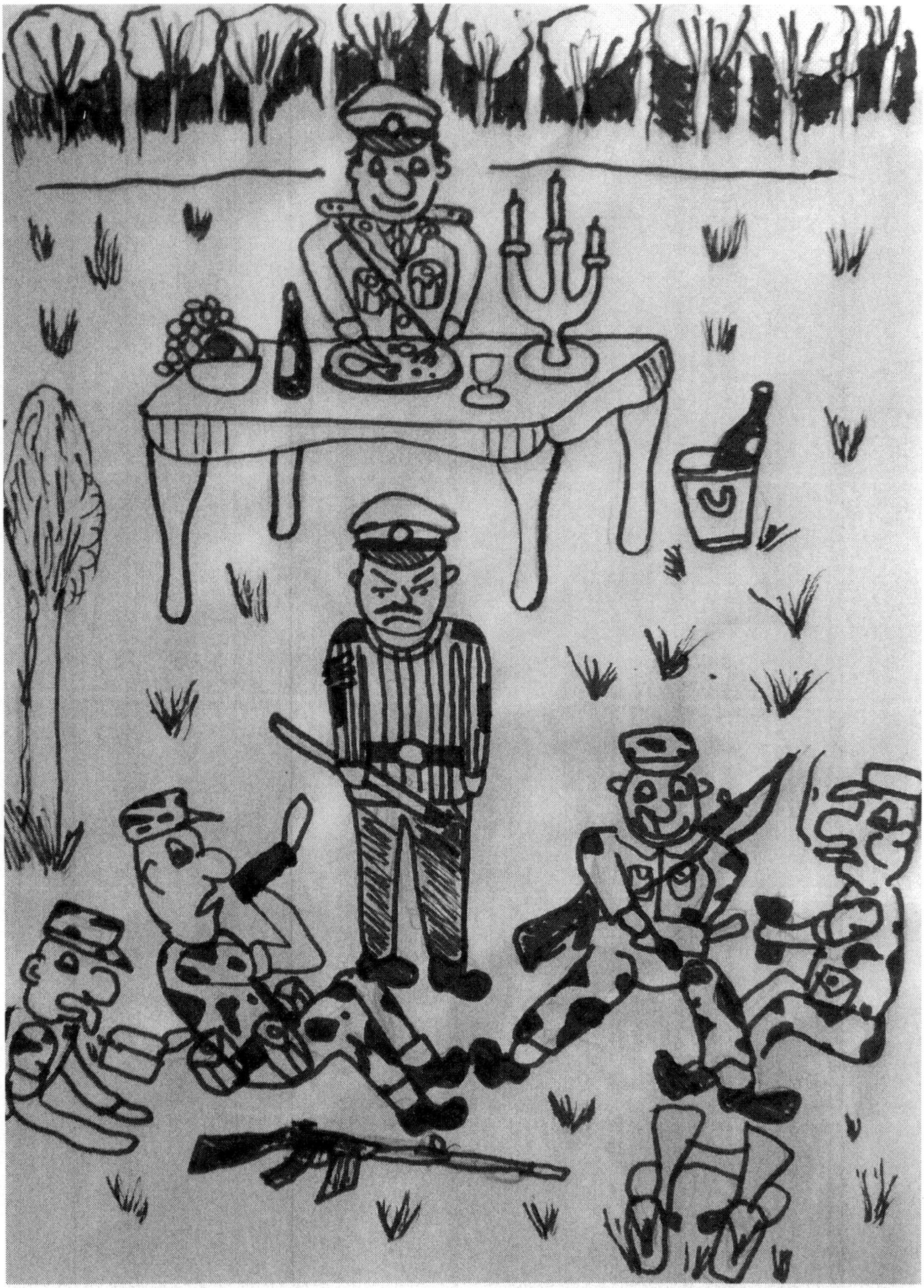

NBC Chamber

In the NBC chamber run by Sergeant Bendly
The training we undertook wasn't very friendly
Off came our respirators
With an awkward clang
And out the door we fucking ran!

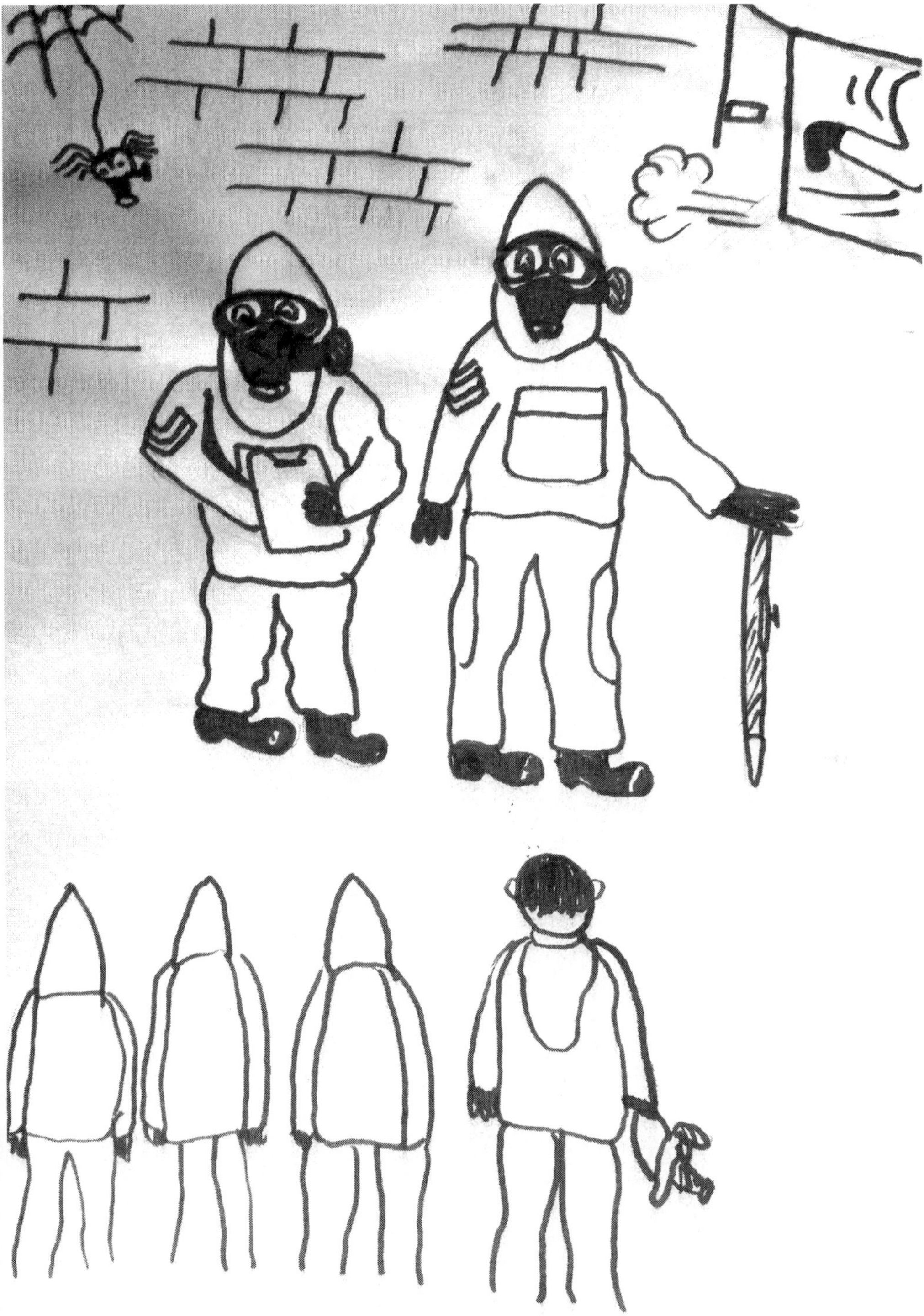

Shitting on Exercise

A soldier on exercise one day
Went into the woods and had a shit of clay
He thought the woods would be decimated
But the compo only made him constipated
He strained, pulled and pushed with dismay
But could only shit a tiny ball of clay that day

Squatting on Salisbury Plain Needing to go
Looking at the plants in an untidy row
Didn't have any toilet roll
But used the leaves like a pro
It wasn't all bad shitting in the snow

Shitting on exercise
Always catches you by surprise
When you need a crap
And you've used your map
It's not ideal but a great compromise

After eating too many fruits
You're shitting long bean shoots
You just don't know
Where to go
So you shit in your best mates boots

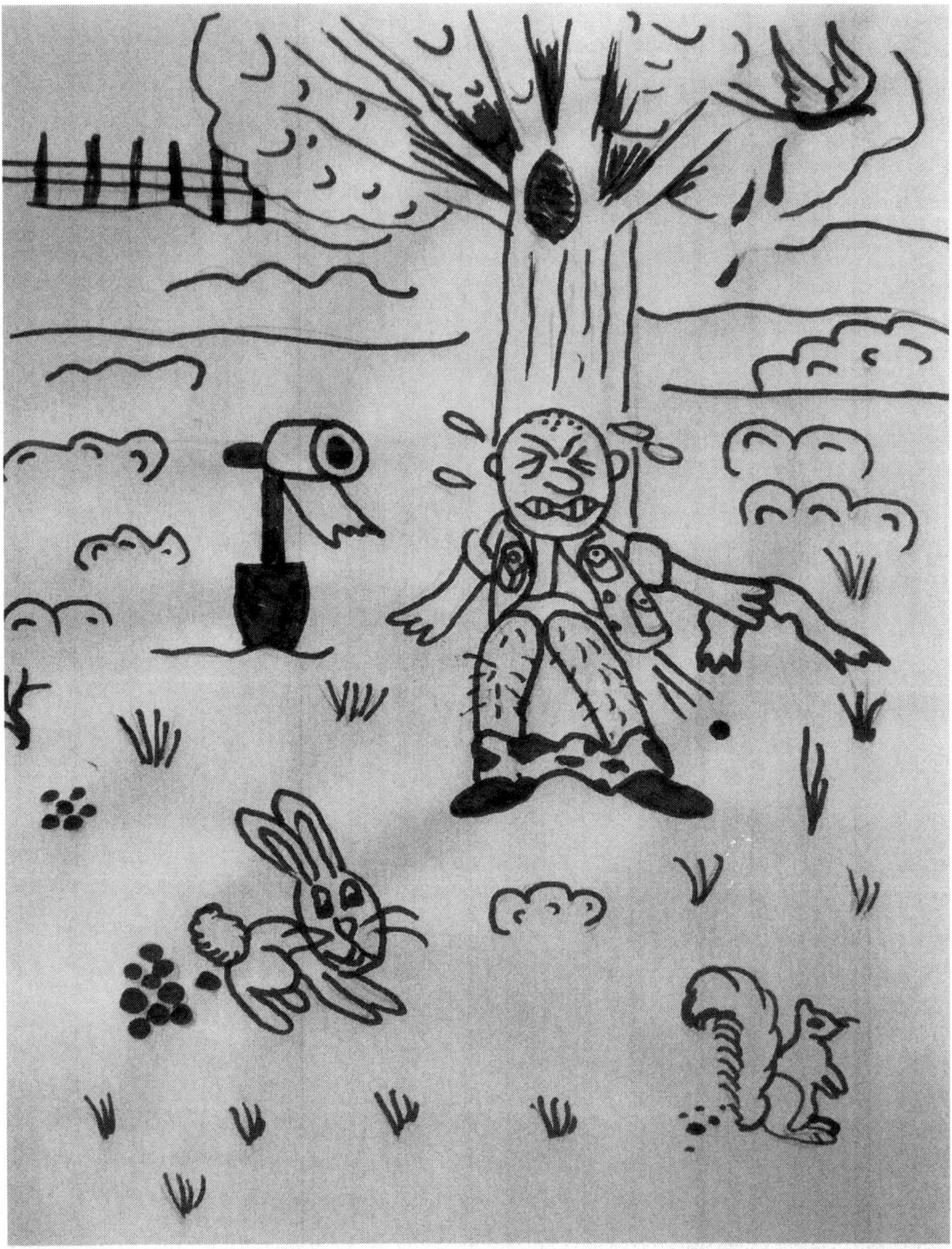

The Sergeant Major In Training

The Sergeant Major in training
Loved to parade when it was raining
He didn't think it funny
When it was sunny
For him it was no longer entertaining

The Sergeant Majors Pace Stick

The Sergeant Majors pace stick was a very useful tool
It would wrap across your knuckles
If you played the fool
It measured the paces
Of shiny boots with straight laces
Other than that it had no use at all

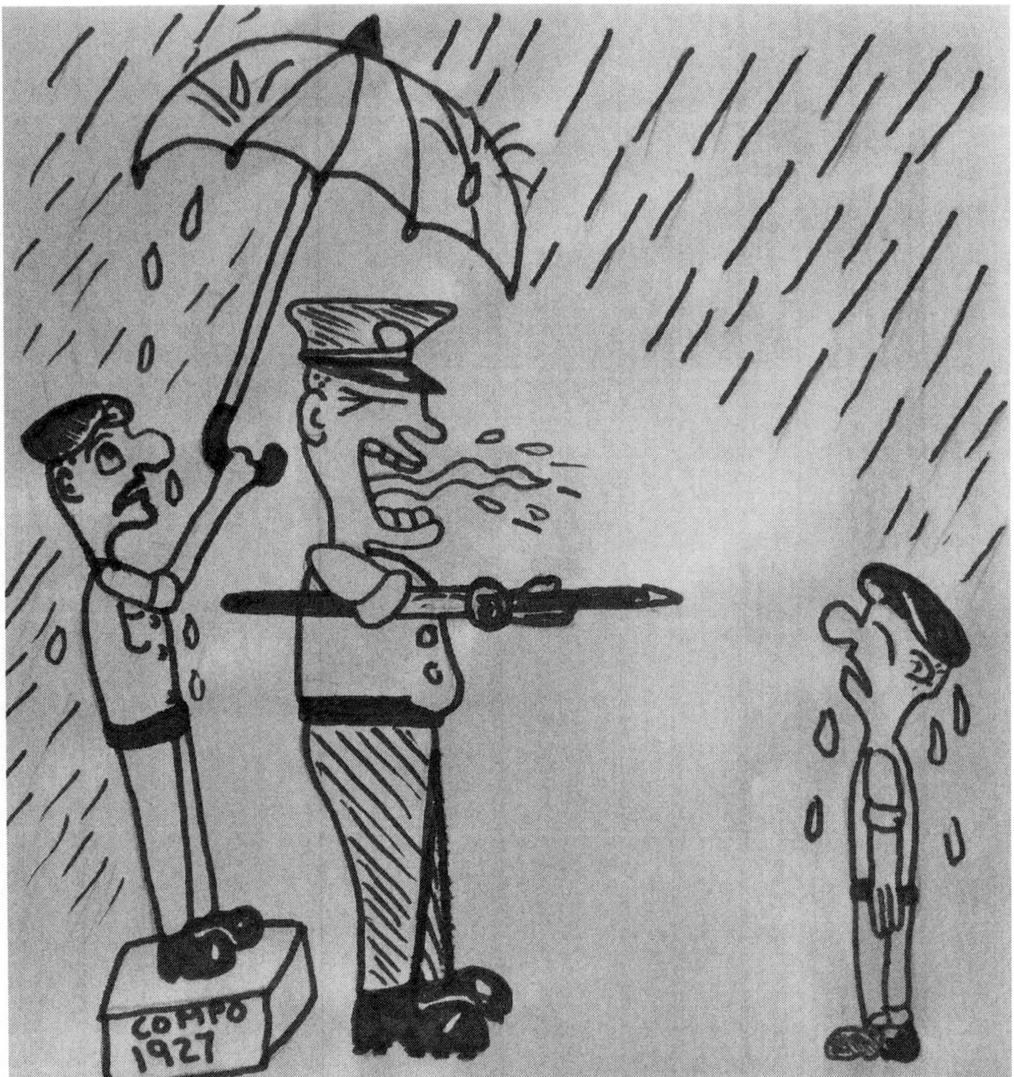
COMPO
1927

The RSM's Grass

The RSM's grass has lots of class
You won't find any grass greener
But if you tread on just a blade
You won't find anybody meaner

If you dare walk on the grass
It's no good disguising your trail
Because he will see you from his office window
And throw you in the fucking jail!

Sitting in the freezing jail
Listening to the winter blizzards
You only come out to cut the grass
With a pair of fucking scissors

RHQ (HEAD SHED)
STRICTL
STAFF CA
ONLY
KEEP OFF
THE GRASS
(CUNT) RSM
?
STA
CAR

The Army Med Centre

The Army Med Centre is a busy hive
That attracts those wanting to skive
After morning inspection
You queue for an injection
And come out barely alive

First Leave

Going on leave was a big deal
Going back home was such a thrill
The first thing to do was get into debt
Cars, stereos or even going to the bookies for a bet

The next thing to do
I'm afraid
Was to go down town and try and get laid
After coming out of the pub being carried
You could return back to camp
Now fully married!

Gambling

In the army you shouldn't gamble
Sitting in a barrack room with a tidy rabble
When you lose all your money on cards
Wasting your time with delinquent retards
It's always best to play Scrabble

Lending Money

Lend us a quid
I hear you say
I'll give it back on pay day

When he says it
In his mind
He has no intention of getting behind

But when pay day comes
And he has paid everybody else
You are left wanting
And on the shelf

ALL PERSONELL
REPORTING SICK
OVER THE WEEKEND
PLEASE FUCKOFF
AFPC
ZCD
GHJ
MNW

Leaving Pets while going on leave In a Regular Unit

A soldier went on annual leave
And left his pets with his mate one Christmas Eve

His mate fed his dog until it exploded with greed

His rabbit was much thinner but that ended up as Christmas dinner

He didn't think his cat was very clean so it ended up in the washing machine

The guinea pig wasn't so big but when he buried it he had to dig

Although the rat was very fit the cat had already eaten it!

The budgie was very brave but he still ended up in a grave

The only one left was a big long snake but when he ran over it, it made him brake

When the soldier came off leave he said, "Thanks mate I knew you'd achieve"

But his mate got out of bed and said "Sorry mate they're all dead"!

Army Bomb Disposal

There was a man in bomb disposal called Fritz
Who blew himself to bits
They found his penis on Venus
And his bollocks on the dining table of the Ritz

Army Ordnance

There was a man in Ordnance called Bill
Who played around with dynamite for a thrill
They found his arms in Vietnam
And his head on the top of a hill

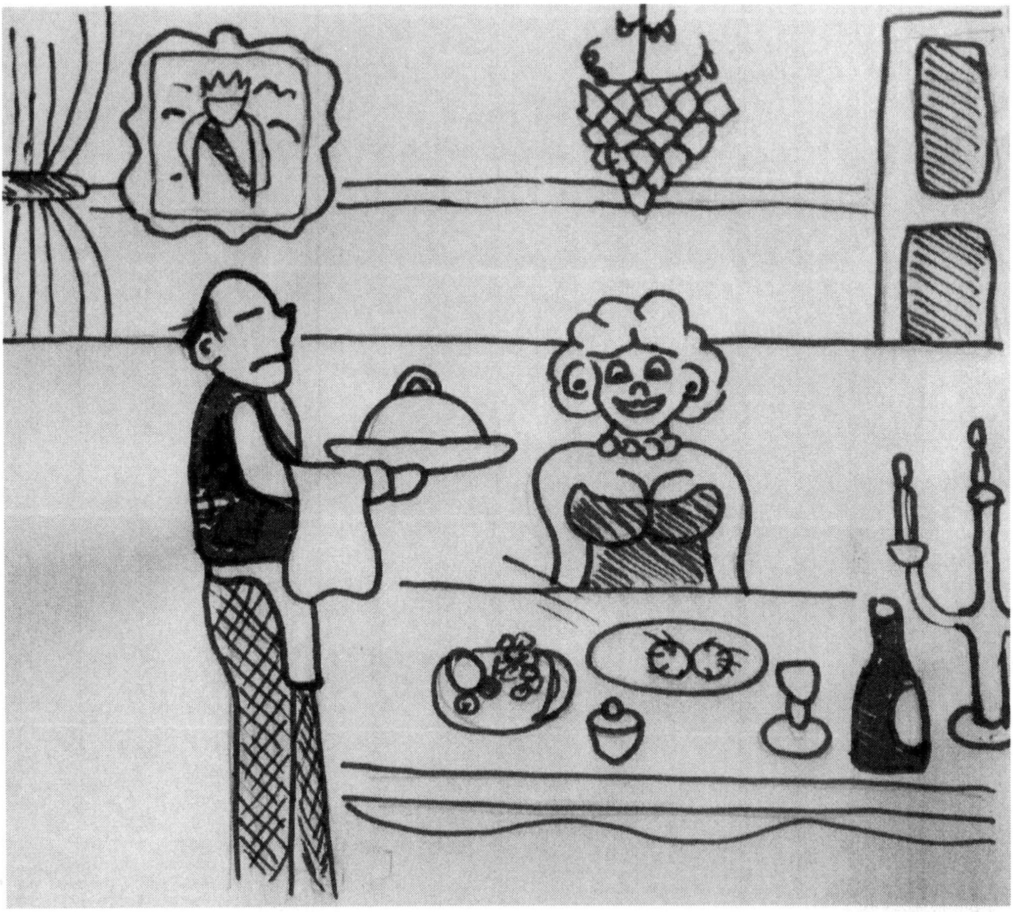

Para

There was a man in the Paras
Who was partial to soup and marrows
When he jumped out of a plane
They thought him insane
Because he would eat his soup with the sparrows

There was a man in the Paras
Who had crazy supernatural powers
He would jump out of a plane
In the pouring rain
And shit bucket loads of flowers

There was a crazy man in the Paras
Who possessed supernatural powers
He would chat up a bird
Give her a turd
And then turn it into a bunch of flowers

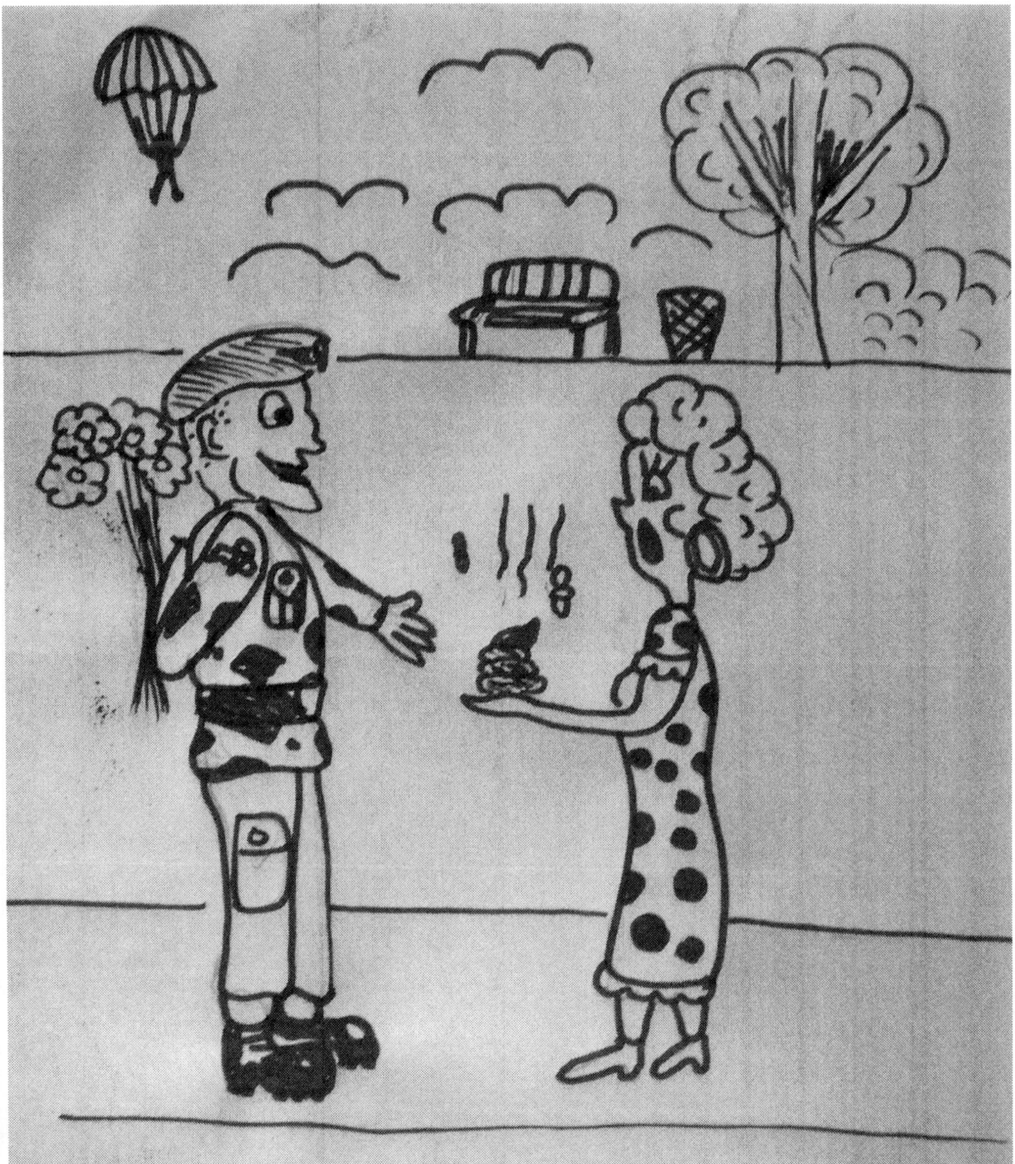

Really Large Corpse

There was a trans in the RLC
It wasn't clear whether they were a he or a she
It was still a mystery in the troop
Whenever this person went for a poop
But all was revealed for all to see
when this person finally went for a pee

Royal Military Police

There was a bastard in the RMP
Who was hated by his whole family tree
There was an exception of one other
Who turned out to be his Mother
But eventually even she had to agree
He was the biggest bastard on the family tree

There was a man in the Royal Military Police
All he could think about was war and peace
He would go out at night
Break up a fight
And then he would turn into a beast

Sgt Major

There was a Sgt Major that loved drill
Who took a psychedelic pill
The parade ground went blurry
And even looked furry
So all he could do was stand still

The Pissed Naafi Taffy

There was a Welsh pisshead in the Naafi
Who thought he was Colonel Gaddafi
Although it was old flannel
He farted like a camel
But really he was just a pissed Taffy

Pioneer Corpse

There was a soldier in the Pioneer Corpse
Who was the fastest labourer you ever saw
He laid the barbwire
like he was on fire
And was always wanting to lay more

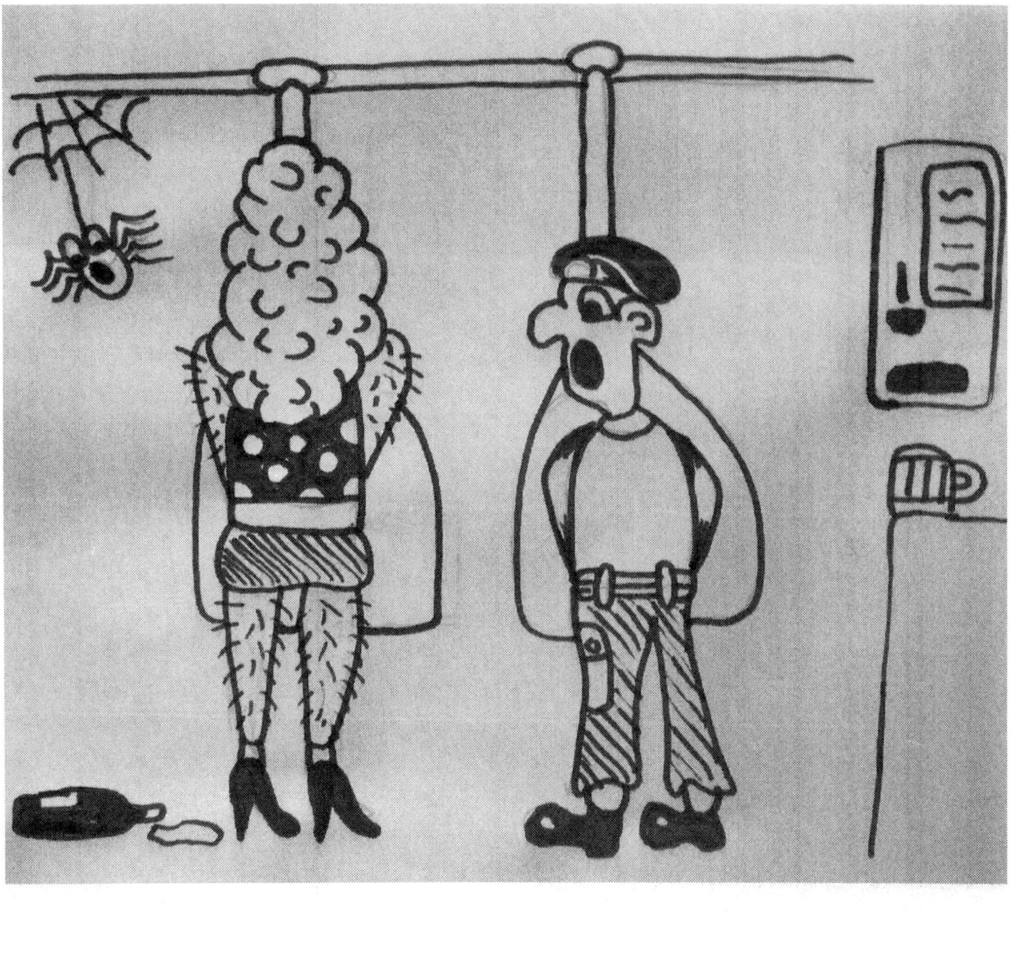

Sapper

There once was a Royal Engineer Sapper
Who was more like a lazy slacker
He built a bridge
That looked more like a fridge
You would have been better off with a cream cracker

Engineer

There was an alcoholic in the Royal Engineers
Who was terrified of poofs and queers
One day one touched his bum
And he had so much fun
That he now prefers them to beers

There was a man in the Engineers
Who liked to go out for a few beers
He got so drunk
He fell out of his bunk
And all he could say was cheers

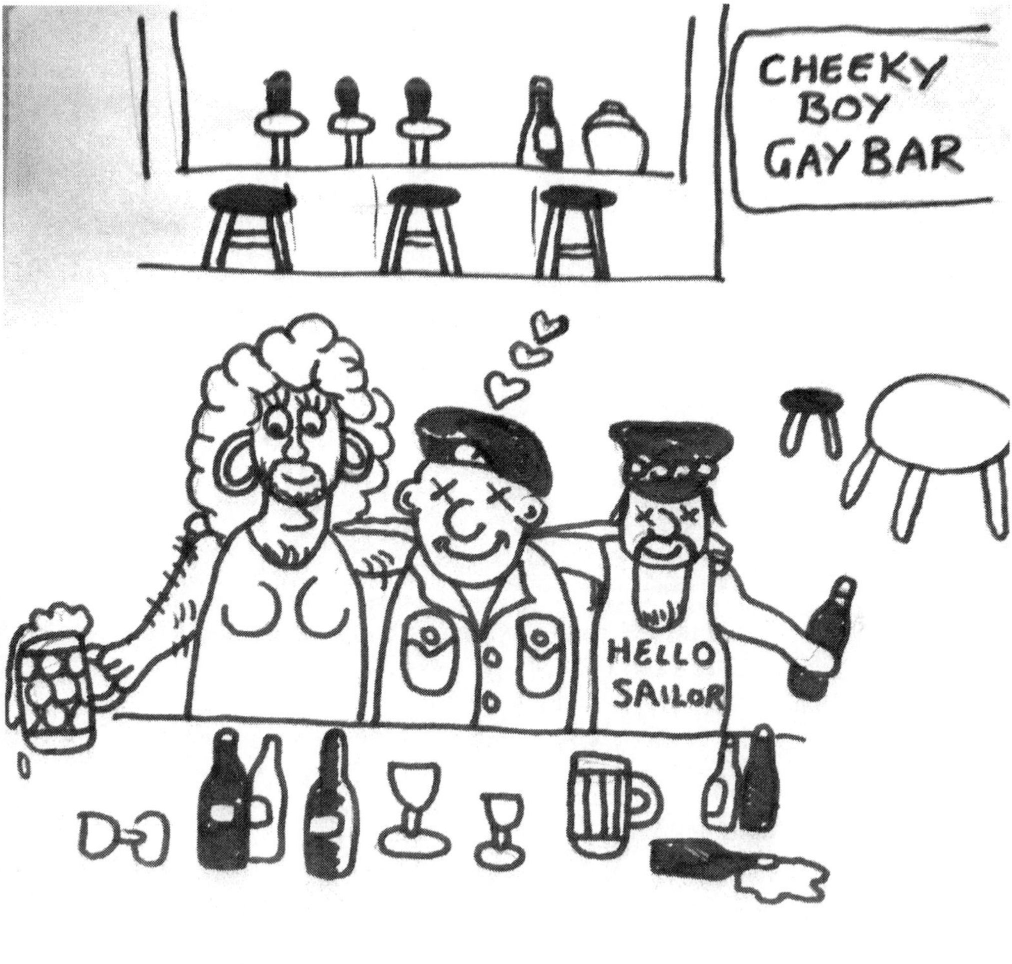
CHEEKY
BOY
GAY BAR
HELLO
SAILOR

RCT Boxers

There was a boxer in the RCT
Who was no higher than your knee
He hit you so hard
you went to lard
Although he was the size of a flea

RCT boxers are the best
Don't be fooled by their crumpled vest
They take on all comers
Including drummers and plumbers
You're sure to come second best

They like to batter everybody with glee
Especially if you are the Infantry
Other regiments entering the ring
Are quickly punched and put in a spin
They don't care if you are big or small
It doesn't matter they beat you all
To be beat by such a fine regiment is not a sin
But you will hit the canvas on your chin

Cultural note: * 10 Regiment RCT was a very well known army boxing regiment in the 1970's/80's
10 Regiment RCT was the best boxing regiment in the whole of the British army In the 1970's it won the British Army Boxing Championship six years running beating all the regiments of the army including all infantry regiments.

There was a boxer from Ten Reg
When pissed would break into the cookhouse for meat and veg
Complaints fell on death ears
And would only end in tears
Because his punch was like being hit with a sledge

Cultural note: * One of 10 Regiment RCT best boxers was well known from coming back from the town pissed and breaking into the cookhouse and cooking food for himself on a regular basis so much so that a new duty was started to guard the cookhouse at night. This new duty changed nothing because he ignored the guard or was just as happy to fight them!

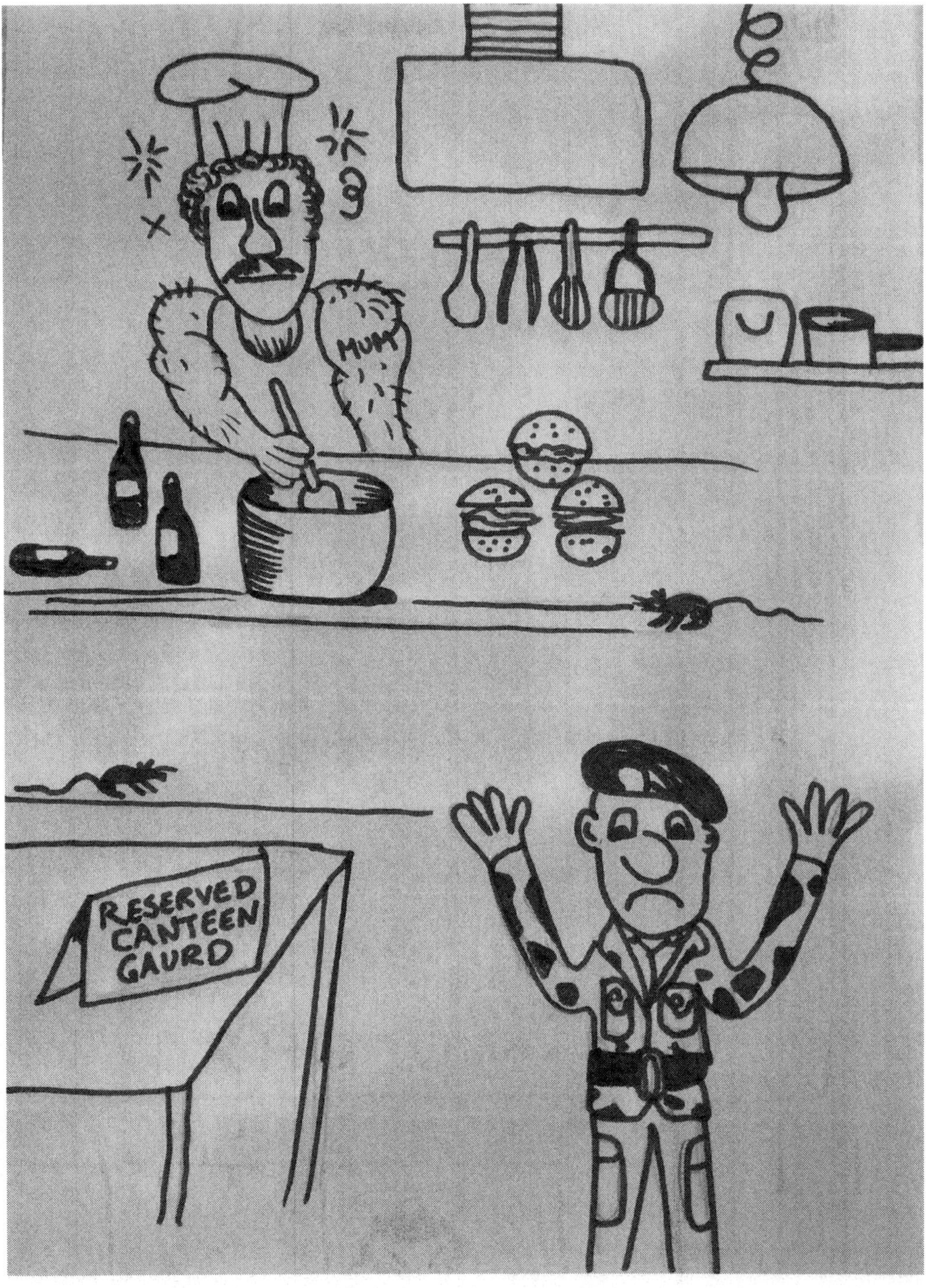
MUM
RESERVED
CANTEEN
GAURD

REME

There was a man in the REME
Who made you very queasy
He changed the oil
with the puss from his boil
And made it look easy peasy

There was a man in the REME
Who seemed to be very sleazy
He serviced the ladies of York
As well as the transport
And rented an apartment above a speakeasy

King's Guard

There was a drill Sergeant in the King's Guard
Who went into a pub looking hard
A fight broke out
The Sergeant gave a shout
And now he's permanently barred

The Coward

A soldier on finishing a guard
Went into a pub thinking he was hard
A fight broke out
The soldier ran out
And now everybody knows he's a lard

Sneaky Beaky

There was a man in the Intelligence Corpse
Who turned out to be a terrible bore
He told boring dits
Till it got on your tits
And nobody could take anymore

Officer

There was an Officer in the Armed Forces
Who liked to skive off doing courses
The Adjutant cottoned on
Thought it was wrong
And now he just mucks out the horses

RAC

There was a man in the Royal Armoured Corpse
Who invented the exploding door
It blew up in his face
Sent him to space
And now he is on the moon floor

Fat Bastard

There was a fat bastard in the Rifles
Who could eat 1000 trifles
He would look in your eyes
And see Naaffi pies
And to him that was a proper eyeful

Sergeants Mess

There was a tight bastard in the Sergeant's Mess
Who would never pay for his booze in a sesh
He was as tight as a fart
And made it such an art
That they put all the booze behind mesh

Naafi Girl

There once was a girl in the Naafi
Who liked to fuck soldiers called Taffy
She would grab their cocks
And give them the pox
And then hide in a different Café

Naafi Bar

There once was a girl in The Naaffi bar
Who liked to shag soldiers in the back of her car
As soon as there was an erection
There was no contraception
So the soldiers had to come in a jar!

Army Stores

In the stores of the Royal Army Ordnance Corpse
Lives a man who keeps the soldiers poor
One day his cigarette lit the gunpowder after a cough
But not before blowing his testicles off!
The soldiers were no longer poor
Because after the explosion there was no fucking door!

Infantry Soldier

There once was an Infantry soldier that couldn't have been more keener
Because he wanted to qualify to be a shithouse cleaner
Instead of camouflage amongst the tree bark
He was more at home scrubbing a skid mark
Such is the life of a dreamer

2nd LT Wong

2nd LT Wong was always wrong
when it came to reading a map
On reflection
 He always went in the wrong direction
So it's fair to say he was crap

SALISBURY
PLAIN
FUCKING MILES AWAY
THIS WAY
UP
-OF BOUNDS
TO MILITARY
RSONNEL
UR LOST

RSM Rollicking

There once was an RSM called Rollicking
Who often liked to give out a bollocking
He went red in the face
While telling you, you were a waste of space
That's why his name was Rollicking

He had the voice of a bear
Freezing you on the spot with his stare
He had breath like death
But with that voice of fire
Louder than the Town Crier
He could also be very fair

He had the shout of a lout
With an almighty clout
And a march as sharp as his starch
If you could stand the pace
He would spit in your face
And bend you in half like an arch

If you saluted him
Things would look very grim
And with a shout, whack and kick
From a pace stick
You could very well be hit on the chin!

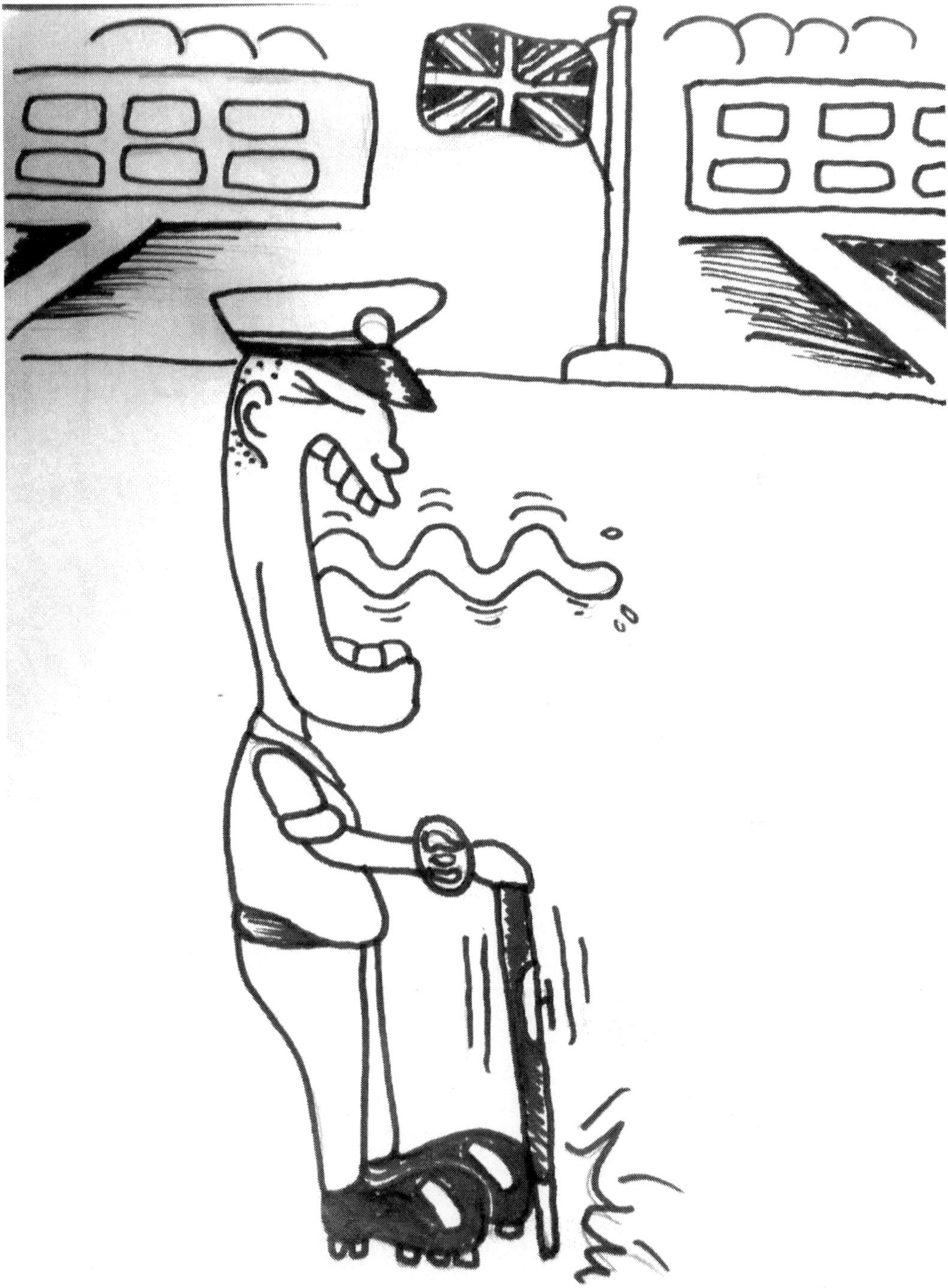

Dit Shit

Dit Shit was called Dit Shit
Because he told shit dits
His dits got you snoring
Because they were boring
It was worse than having the shits

Staff Car Driver

There was a staff car driver from afar
That liked to fuck hookers in the Generals car
Sitting in the back one day
The General looked in dismay
Chewing on what he thought was a bar of Snickers
It turned out the General was chewing on a pair of whore's knickers!

Royal Corpse of Transport

A Driver in the RCT did something rather sleazy
He dipped the clutch
And split his crotch
And now it's rather breezy

Drink Driver

An RCT driver with a very big lorry
Did something one day that would make him very sorry
After hitting and scraping all of those cars
He wished he hadn't gone in all of those bars!

After standing in front of the CO treading the boards
He had no choice but to accept his award
He couldn't deny hitting and scraping all of those cars
And now he will be seeing a different kind of bars

The Grenade Range

There was a man on the Grenade range
Who seemed to be acting rather strange
He pulled out the pin
Stuck it under his chin
And now his face has been rearranged

Stagging On

As a soldier stagged on the gate
He wondered what he had done to deserve such a fate
As he looked into the warm Guard Room
He could see a prisoner pushing a broom
The soldier dreamt of coming off the gate and having a brew
But his stomach said otherwise and he wanted a poo
As he went into the freezing sentry box
It was only a stage up from having the pox
This sentry box was no bog
But it didn't stop the soldier from leaving a log

Range Day

On Range Day there was no fuss
You left camp on a big white bus
As you left the camp gate
You would be sitting next to your best mate
Who would be squeezing a zit full of puss

Arriving at the Range gate
Would be the start of a big balls ache
Taking it in turns of shooting and in the butts
You would be thinking of last night with the booze and the sluts

Gladly stopping for lunch you sighed Phew!
Only to find out lunch was Range Stew!
There was no way of taking your pick
Just a mess tin full of Range stew sick

Cracking on in the afternoon shooting and butts
Now you were thinking of tonight's booze and sluts!
Sitting in the butts pasting up thinking am I a trained exterminator
No! you're a trained wallpaper painter and decorator!

After all the shooting has finished
And all the targets are diminished
All the army tired faces
Collect up all the empty cases
This fine nation
Just needs to make one final declaration
What do you have to say?
 You hear the range commander purr
I have no live rounds or empty cases in my possession sir!

After a final clamour on the big white bus
Now there is plenty of fuss
For a final chat and a snooze

The big nightly hunt starts
For the birds and the booze!

Buckingham Palace

There once was a Guardsman called Geordie
Who went to Buckingham Palace for an orgy
When he got there
He stripped bollock bare
But there was nobody there but a Corgi

Aldershot Recruit

There was a recruit from Aldershot
A peaceful man he was not
He ran up a hill
And went for the kill
And ended in blood and snot

Careless Officer

There was an officer from Sandhurst
Who seemed to be permanently cursed
He fell down a tank track
And broke his back
And now he is forever nursed

One Sausage Chef

There was an army chef called Jeff
That only ever gave you one sausage
This seemed rather unfair
So he was hit with a chair
And now he only offers porridge

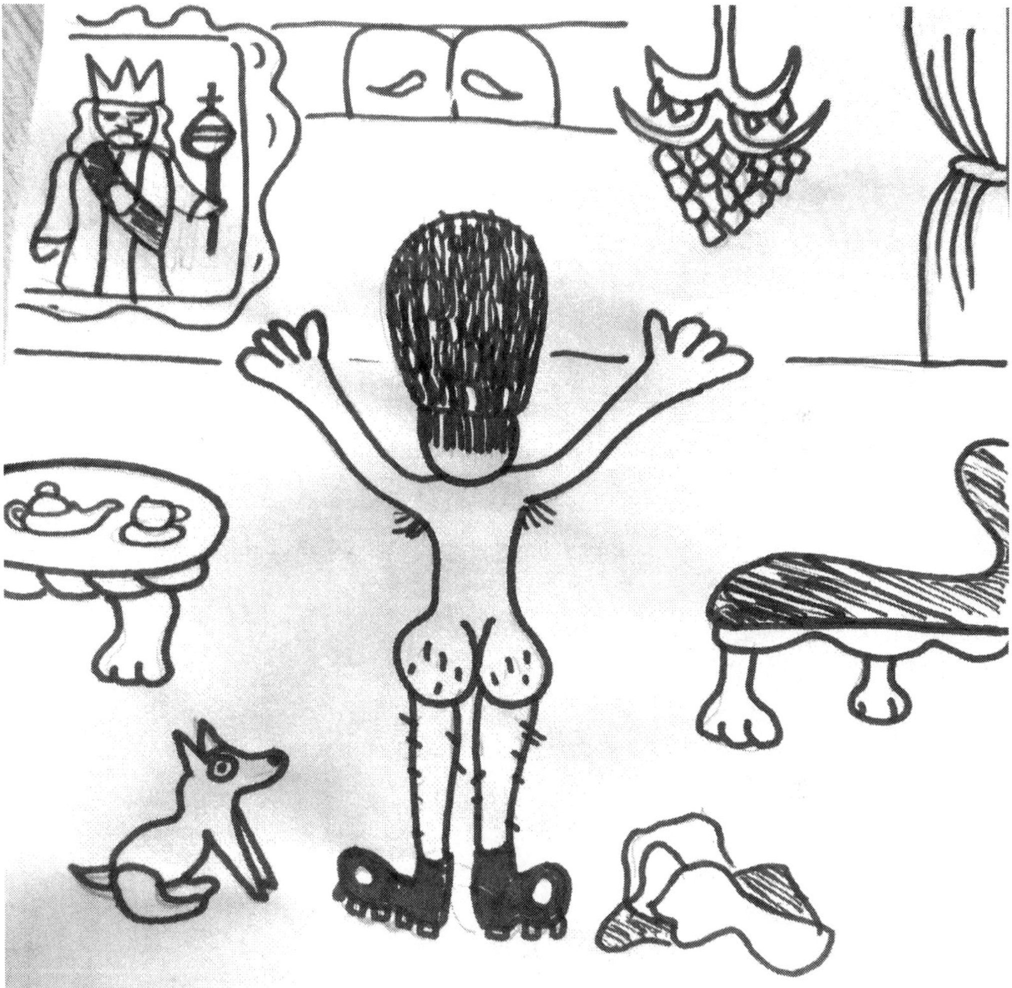

Garrison

There was a corporal in the Garrison
That liked to wave around his cock for comparison
When he drunk too much beer
He would stick it in your ear
So it was best to hide in a Saracen

CO's Daughter

There was a Lance Corporal called Walter
Who was fucking the CO's daughter
The CO was wise
So it's no surprise
That Walter was posted to Gibralter

Pad Shagger

There was a pad shagger called Sythe
Who was fucking everybody's wife
Although he had charm
He did lots of harm
So the lads cut off his bollocks with a knife!

Army Medic

There was an Army Medic called Milly
Who would only inspect you when chilly
When you stripped bare
She would give a disapproving stare
Especially at your freezing willy!

Shitting The Bed

There was a Soldier called Ned
Who would often shit the bed
He awoke one morning
Without any warning
With a shit too big for the bed

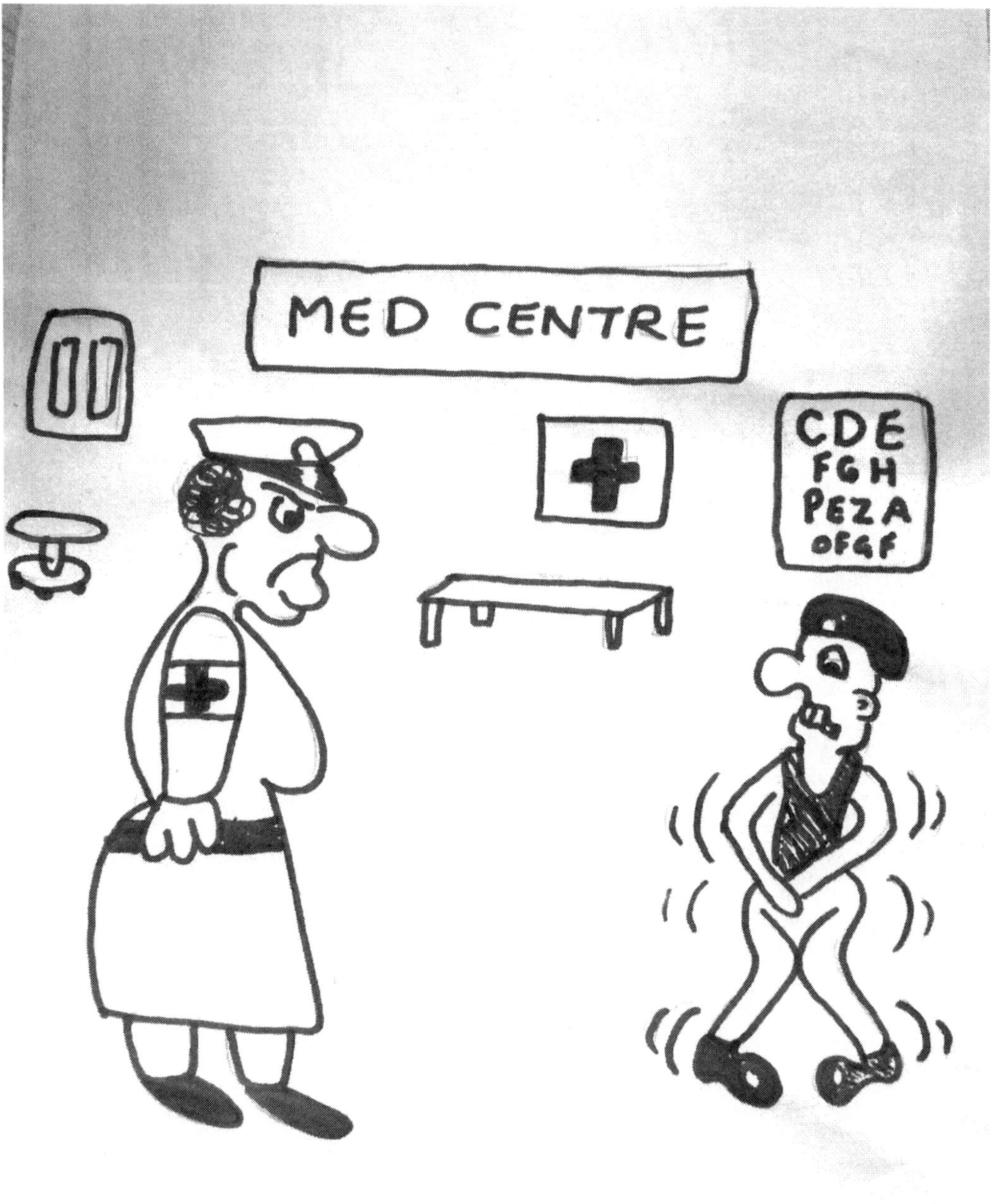
MED CENTRE
CDE
FGH
PEZA
OFGF

Rupert

There was a Rupert with a dog called Fritz
That seemed to have the permanent shits
When the officer ironed his shirt
The dog would squirt
Leaving all the other officers in fits

Getting Busted

There was an NCO called crusted
Who was always getting busted
He thought it exciting
To get arrested for fighting
And again his rank has been adjusted

Army Dentist

There was a Colonel in the Dental Corpse called Paul Teeth
Who could give your gums real grief
If you needed a crown
He would file them down
With no sign of anaesthetic or relief

Walter Mitty

Every Regiment has a Walter Mitty
That can tell the most outrageous ditty
When his mates call him out
He collapses pretending gout
But that won't win him any pity

New Posting

There was a soldier that was a Dragoon
That was supposed to be posted to Cancun
He upset his boss
And to his cost
He got posted to a fucking Monsoon

There was a soldier called Patrick
Who dreamed of being posted to Maastricht
He filled out the form
As was the norm
But ended up posted to Catterick

10 REGIMENT RCT

Head Shed

There was a soldier called Fred Dredd
Who often shit by the head shed
When he was about
The RSM would shout
Be sure to fucking look where you tread!

Artillery

There was a Gunner in the Artillery called Barris
Who was fucking two sisters from Paris
They were both big hits
Because they had huge tits
But he preferred the one with the big Harris

Trog

In the RCT They're called a Trog
They're treated three levels lower than a swamp frog
Taking soldiers from A to B
They're seen as a Rickshaw, cab or Taxi
But underneath they know the truth
Everybody's grateful
Of their canvas roof!

Pioneer Corpse

The Pioneer Corpse
Were not there to adore
They provided the army labour in times of war

Digging holes erecting fences and barbwire
You couldn't wish for finer men to hire
What a sight
Working day and night
They were always ready to stop work and fight

Corporal Fry

This is the story of Lance Corporal Fry
Who fucked all the girls in the regiment
Until they were dry
This was enough to turn them all gay
Making it difficult for him to find a new lay

Drying Room Thief

There was a soldier called Private May
Who stole all the clothes from the drying room one day
When the lads saw him in their clothes
He was quick to have it on his toes
But later on in the bar
The lads covered his bollocks with feathers and hot tar

The Camp Car Dealer

There once was a REME Sgt called Podgy
Who sold cars on camp that were very dodgy
Each car came with a curse
And was permanently stuck in reverse
With plenty of leaks that were splodgy

Provost Sergeant

There once was a Provost sergeant called Snail
That was keen to throw everybody in the Jail
He would come out of his lair
March you up and down the Square
Until you were chin strapped and pale

The Army Disco

The army disco was rife
With the ugliest birds you'd seen in your life
They had tattooed tits
Covered in zits
But they could still end up as your wife

Lieutenant Candy

There was a Lieutenant called Candy
Who was popular in the Mess for being randy
Although very petite
She had a face like mincemeat
And a twat like The Rio Grande

Popular Officer

There was an officer called Sandy
Who made the lads very randy
When lifting her kit
She showed a bit of her tit
But only when she'd been on the brandy

The Army Med Centre

The Army Med Centre was full of Docs
That could only diagnose the pox
If you went in with the flu
It was no good to you
Because they only dealt in blobby cocks

Army Catering Corpse

In The Army Catering Corpse there was a cook called Ralph
Who ate a ten-man ration pack all to himself
When he farted
The Regiment parted
And you could smell it from North to South

Warrant Officer Slop Jockey

There once was a WO2 Slop Jockey
Who thought he was rather cocky
He thought he was the best
Because he wore the crest
But he didn't know his quiche from his broccoli

Jock Drinker

There was a Jock in the Naafi bar called Mc Gable
That could drink an entire regiment under the table
He was once in the dock
For drinking a brewery's entire stock
But I think that part was just fable

Elf on Exercise

There was a soldier on exercise with a weak bladder
Who was cornered by a fucking great adder
The soldier was the size of an elf
Always pissing himself
So could only escape with a ladder

The Regimental Wanker

This is the story of Private Banking
Who just couldn't stop wanking
He wanked on the parade square everyday
So everybody thought he must be gay

He wanked in the cookhouse on various dates
So it was recommended not to lick the plates

He wanked on the vehicle park
Even though it was not dark

He wanked in the Sergeants Mess one night
But burnt his bollocks on an electric light

He was heard in the armoury wanking calling out "Carol"
Only to be found with his cock down a barrel
He still didn't come clean and was even seen
Rubbing his balls up and down a magazine

He wanked in the Officers Mess one day
And came in the big brass ashtray

He was only fit for pushing a broom
Because the only place he didn't wank
Was in his fucking room!

Army Pay Office

There was a corporal in the Pay Corpse
Who bashed the calculator until his fingers were red raw
If you went in the pay office asking for a rise
You had a better chance of doing the lottery and winning the main prize
It was always a mistake showing any expertise
As this only resulted in a pay freeze

Royal Signals

There was a Signal man that was quite dumb
Who liked to play on the radio just for fun
When it came to a grid reference
He had no preference
So now we're blown to kingdom come!

Getting a Tattoo in an Army Garrison Town In the 1970's/80's

An army recruit whilst sitting on the loo
Was inspired that day to get a tattoo

His lack of courage was extremely severe
So after drinking a large quantity of beer
He entered the parlour
Finding a tattooist with a suspicious sneer

The tattooist could see through the recruit's pretence
But was really only concerned that he had pounds shillings and pence

He nervously waited his turn with the lads
Sitting in the waiting room smoking shit loads of fags

When his turn came he put down his hood
Stalling for time he asked the tattooist was he any good?

The tattooist replied "I'll do my best, now let's see that skinny chest"
The recruit sat back squeezing the chair
The tattooist dug the needles in without a care

Looking at the tattooist and client
From outside it wasn't fully clear
Who had actually drunk the most beer

The tattooist concentrating with blood dripping hands
The recruit sitting with empty beer cans

Neither was willing to give an inch
But the tattooist was winning with his very firm pinch

The tattooist's nails were covered in ink
At that point the recruit farted there was an almighty stink

The recruit fixed his gaze on a giant biblical painting
It was all he could do to stop himself fainting

After all was said and done
The recruit got up with a very numb bum

All his mates had already gone
While the dressing was firmly put on

The tattooist was pleased with what he had done
The recruit looked down
Just three letters that said "MUM"

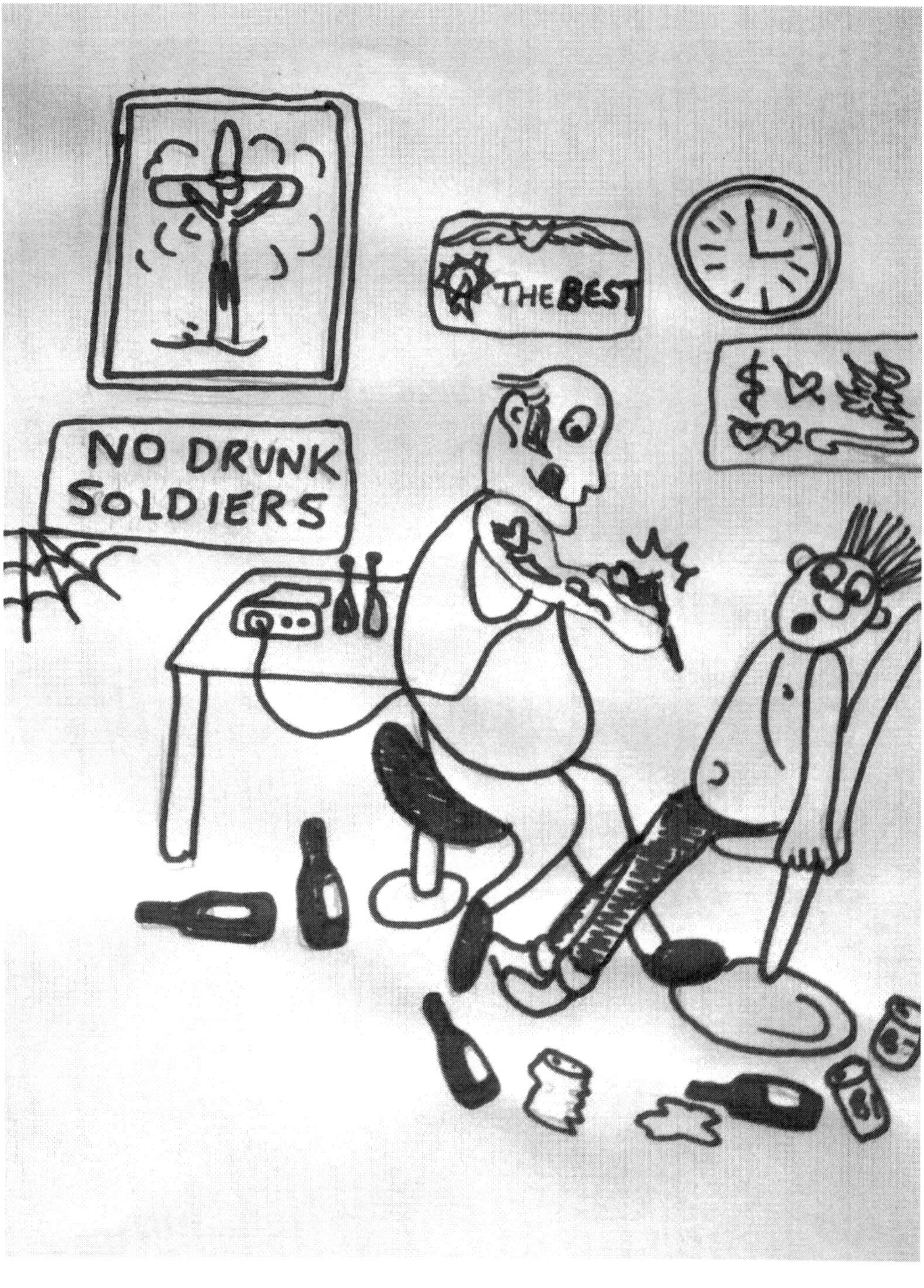
THE BEST
NO DRUNK SOLDIERS

Winter Exercises

Winter exercises were always much fun
You could freeze your bollocks off in the winter sun

Shagging a sheep at dawn
Was the only sure way to keep warm

Only to be disturbed by the Sergeant Major
Shouting "That's fucking unnatural porn!"

Stuck in a frozen trench
With mildew and stench

There was only compo
And one dead crow
To keep you on the go

Why did they always shout "STAND TOO"
At the precise moment you wanted a smoke, brew and poo

Summer Exercises

Summer exercises were always so much fun
You could pass out from exhaustion under the midday sun

Last night we were on a full beer sesh
And now we are in full battle dress

With an empty water bottle made of enamel
You were loaded up with a back-pack like a fucking camel

Too much kit on for masturbation
You will die first of dehydration

With no more food and no more water
We are ready for the fucking slaughter

Chin strapped with double cramp
Let's get on the four tonner and fuck off back to camp!

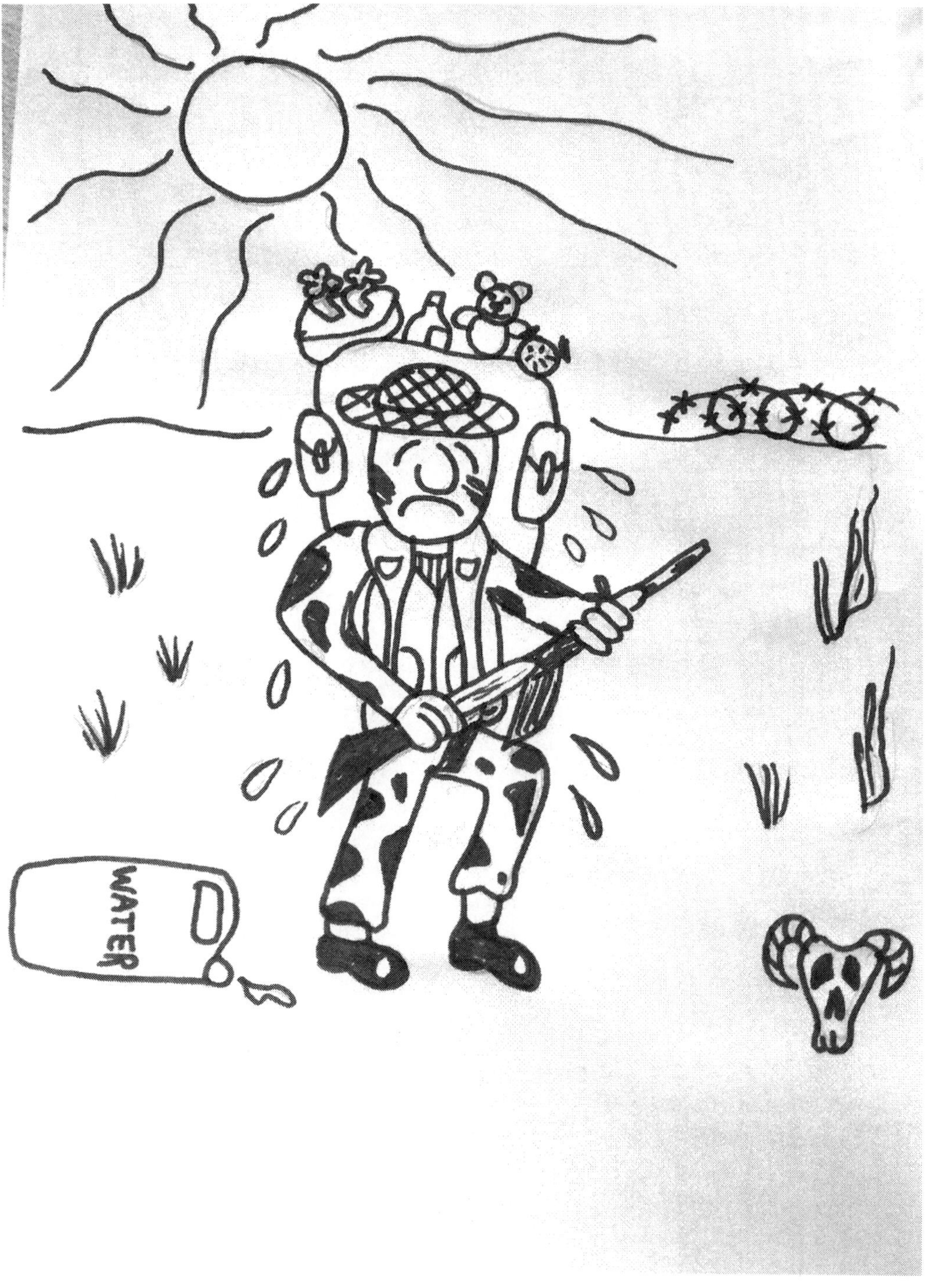
WATER

Down Town

The squaddies went down town for the night
It was bound to end up with beer and a terrible fight

They drunk and drunk until they were wrecked
The night wouldn't be finished until somebody was decked

There was somebody in the corner giving a long and hard stare
And then there were tables and chairs flying everywhere

After the first person was dropped
The music went silent and was stopped

The DJ had stopped playing
And civilians were praying

Many people were on their arse
Sitting on a pile of broken glass

When the last punch had landed
By a man who was right handed
The lights of the bar came on

After everybody parted it was clear who started
They were definitely in the wrong
But it wasn't a Squaddie or anybody
It was a bird who looked like King Kong

She had a face like a mutt
With a massive beer gut
And a face as ugly as sin
But she wouldn't hesitate to hit you on the chin
With her big fat strut
Somebody had called her a slut
And that's what made the fight begin!

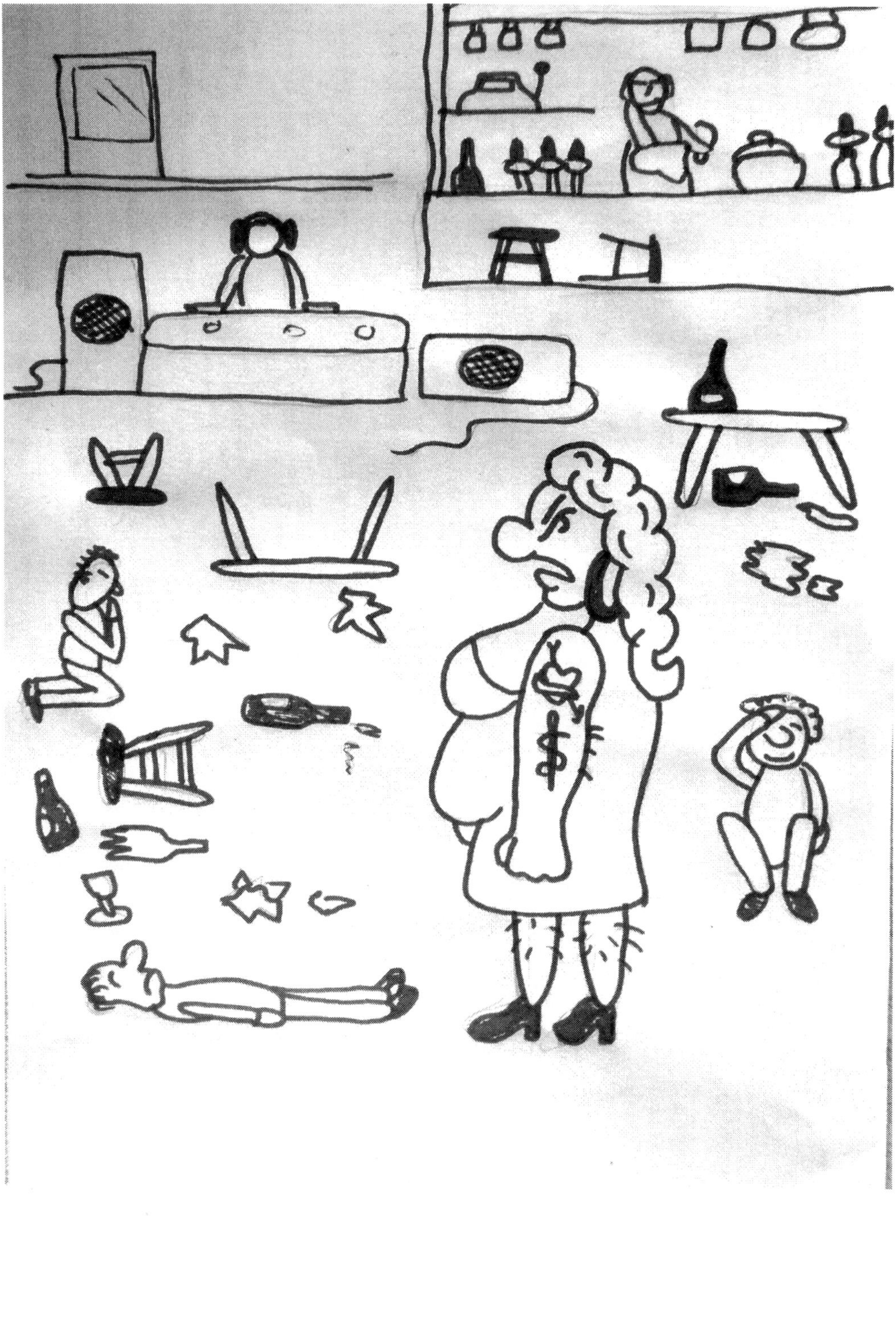

Clap Clinic

Down at the Med Centre reporting sick
Is no fun with a blobby dick

Sitting in the waiting room along with the family's
Out comes the medic shouting out with a cheer
"Here's your VD results you've got the all clear!"

With a red face you carefully tread
Past your colleagues wives having lost all street cred

At the next troop piss up you eat Naafi pies
Avoiding all contact with the family wives

But after a fair few
You think it is wise
To start cracking VD jokes at the family wives

Fighting with RMP's

There was an RMP who was a dick
He got punched in the face and got a fat lip
In the heat of the fight
The soldier who did it lost his shoe
But the RMP now looks like a monkey from the fucking zoo!

Weekend In Amsterdam

There were some red light girls who seemed more superior
Although their working parts were definitely more inferior
What they had was contagious
The Medics wouldn't have forgave us
What was needed was an injection in the posterior

Christmas

There was a soldier called O'Racka
Who fucked a Christmas cracker
He turned out the light
Found it too tight
But now it's much slacker

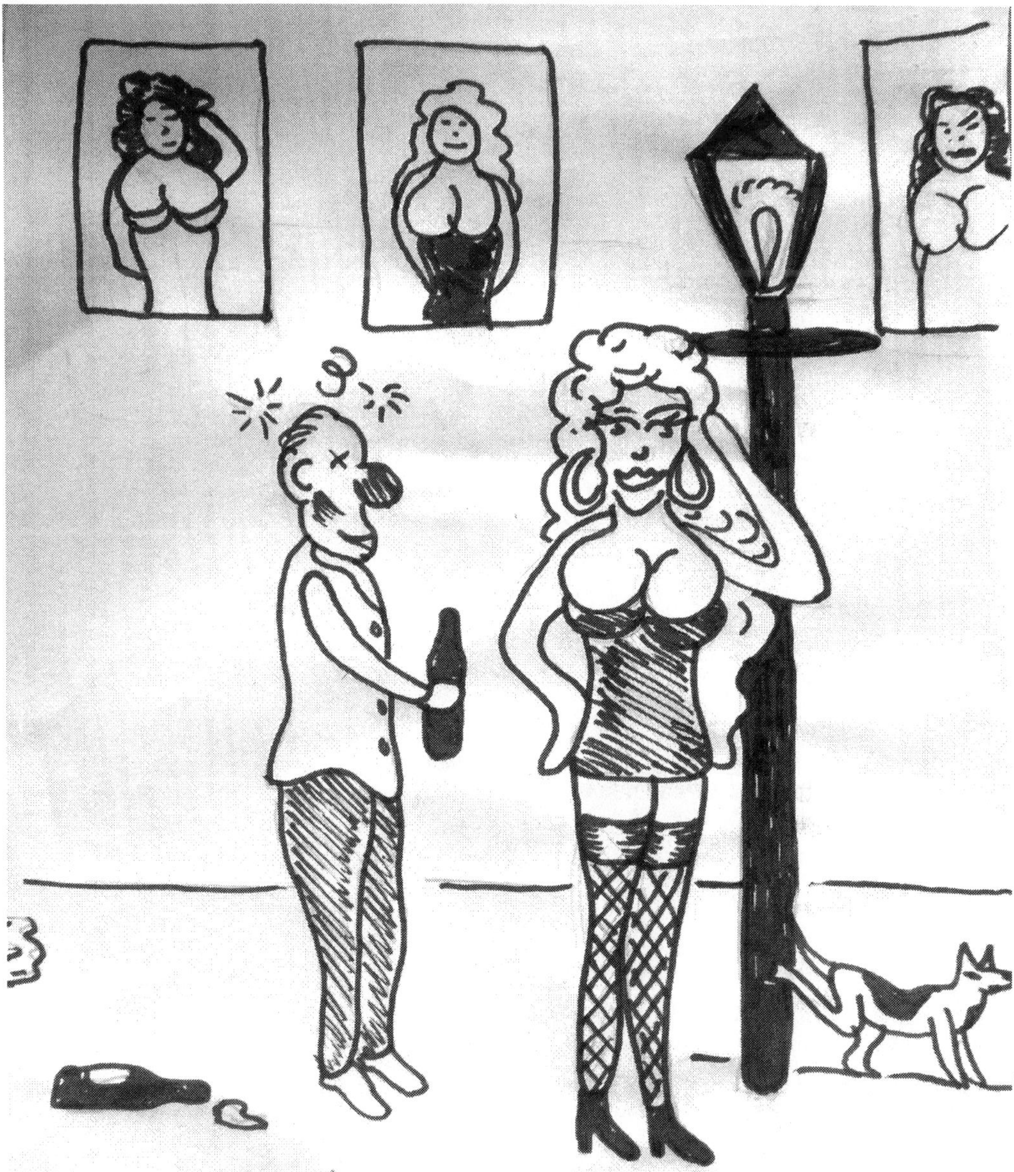

Sniper

There once was a sniper who was a good shot
Who totally lost the plot
He would fire at cows and sheep
While the range officer was asleep
The definition of sanity he was not

Marksman

There was a marksman from Timbuktu
Who woke up one afternoon for a piss and a brew
He looked all around for something to chew
But as he was in the range butts
There was only wood and glue

Grab a Granny Night

When a young soldier is desperate for fanny
He may consider a granny
With bingo wings
And double chins
Anything's better than a tranny

Unemployed

There was an unemployed recruit from Liverpool
Who wasn't lazy as a rule
He didn't want to join the army and live in a hole
But decided it was better than being on the dole

Glaswegian Kiss

There was a Glaswegian soldier called Trowels
Who was always getting in rows
If you called his wife a slut
You could expect a head butt
And then he would rip out your bowels

Young Officer

There was a young officer from Timbuktu
Who was officer material through and through
When it came to map reading
Because of the inbreeding
The troops found themselves in Peru

Not put off the young officer did scoff
And made himself a brew
Now refreshed and chilled
They went through a minefield
And he was blown back to Timbuktu

Royal Navy

There was a very capable lad from Timbuktu
Who thought he would join the army for something to do
He went to the Royal Navy recruiting first
This was to be for better or worst
And without further ado
He found himself in a battleship crew

This was very underhand on the Navy's part
The lad was hoping for a better start
The lad was now wishing he was back in Timbuktu
And all it had cost the Navy was a chat and a brew

Pissed Squaddies

Three pissed squaddies sitting on a wall
Looking out for tits big or small
Looking for thrills
Drinking Pils
But in an all male barracks
They saw fuck all

The Worst Shot In The Regiment

The worst shot in the regiment was Geordie Jarrow
He couldn't hit a sparrow
He was one of a kind
Half blind
And better off with a kids bow and arrow

Geordie

There was a Geordie from Jarrow
Who kept his giant bollocks in a wheel barrow
He didn't give a fuck
When the wheelbarrow got stuck
Because the Guardroom door was too narrow

The Thickest Bastard In The Regiment

The thickest bastard in the regiment was private Fallow
Who's intellect was quite shallow
Ordered to get bedding and webbing
He came back with a trifle and a marshmallow

The Most Intelligent Man In The Army

The most intelligent man in the army was WO1 Spivvy
Who certainly was no divvy
When asked by a private so bold
Of all the ranks best to hold
He immediately replied a Civvy

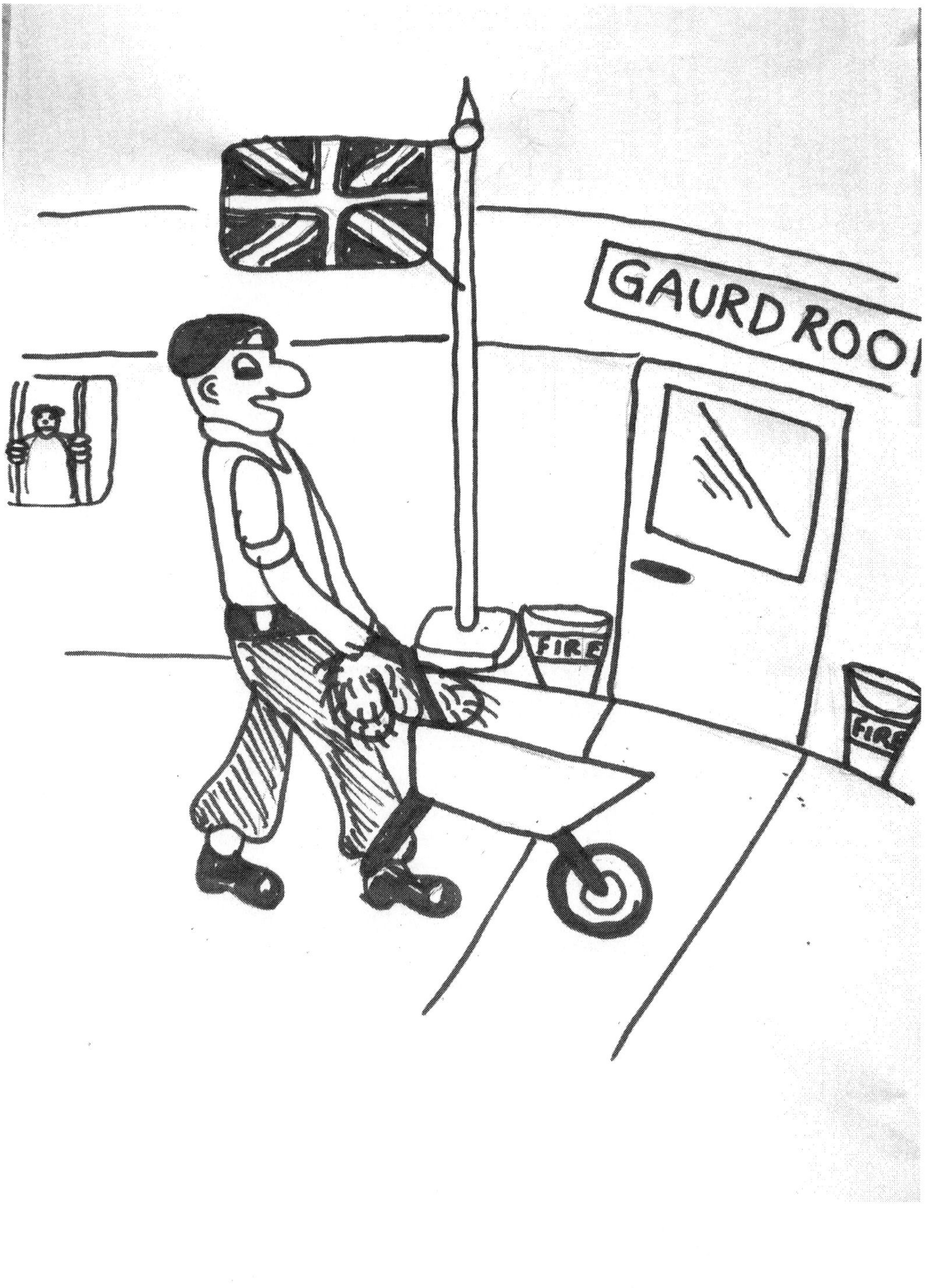
GAURD ROO
FIRE
FIRE

Top Brass Inspection

The General is coming to inspect
All those present and correct
Painted kerbstones
Scrubbed porcelain thrones
Enthusiasm we must inject

Anybody outspoken or looking like a Fromage Frais
Will be hidden and kept out of his way that day

The staff car arrives
The lame and sick skive
The CO flaps
While the RSM craps
What a sight for sore eyes

The General inspects the accommodation block
Under a bed he finds a porno mag and a dirty sock
A Sergeant who is very stressed
Looks at the General unimpressed

While the General is inspecting polished floors
The troop Corporal opens the locker doors
All the NCO's are frustrating
As the culprit is in the locker masturbating
While as the General can't take anymore

Friday Afternoons

On Friday afternoon
We are promised the moon
Hoping to knock off early
And find a girly
We are more likely to be pushing a broom!

It turned out to be all lies
The sports afternoon promised
Has disappeared in front of our eyes

This is our fate
Instead of early we are now very late
The senior NCO wants a row
And still working he says:
"Your'e in your own time now!"

Army Barmy (Or career regrets?)

There is a Bloke in our troop who is totally army barmy
There would be no problem if he wasn't so smarmy

He likes to bull his boots to such a shine
When he's not looking I try and swop them for mine

On a Friday night when everybody's down town
He stays in camp in his dressing gown

On a Saturday night he stays in pressing his kit
While we all think what a tit!

While we are all dreaming of fondling female pubic hair
He is dreaming of marching up and down the square

While we are on orders for some petty farce
He is licking the Sergeant Majors arse

With all this chaos and commotion
He receives more promotion

Many years later
While working as a waiter
I was skint and in redemption
While he was driving a Mercedes
And drawing an army pension

Now I'm an old sweat with no regret
It's hard to say which way was best
In the end it matters not
As long as we can all jest

Civvy Street

After leaving the army with marching feet
You find yourself in civvy street
After many exercises
And early rises
In civvy street you must now compete

In the army bulling the block like a cleaner
You dream of civvy street
Thinking the grass must be greener

In the army marching across the marshes
You may have been thinking of civvy street
With rose tinted glasses

But now you have left the army
It's not all great and sunny
All of a sudden you look in your pocket
To find you have no money

You no longer have to listen to the Sergeant Majors gob
But you do have to go out and get a fucking job!

Thanks again for reading my shit dits
I hope at least a couple had you in fits
If you are offended
And feel they should be amended
I'll put in more shits, zits and clits!

The following titles are available as Notebooks, Internet Password Books And Any Year Diaries Search: Squaddie Brand Publishing on amazon by Regiment

Notebook, Internet Password Books and Any Year Diaries

The Most Awesome Bastard In The British Army — by Ima Leg End

The Most Awesome Beardy Bastard In The British Army — by Pte Hare

The Biggest Party Animal In The Army — by Lou Nattic

The Most Handsome Bastard In The British Army — by Ima Leg End

The Most Awesome Sniper In The Army — by Mark Smann

The Most Awesome Driver In The Army — by Wills Mann

The Most Awesome Clerk In The Army — by Ivan Otherbrew

The Most Awesome PTI In The British Army — by Jim Nasti

Most Awesome Drill Instructor In The British Army — by Mark Tyme

The Most Awesome Dog Handler In The Army — by Al Seyshan

Don't Fuck With An Army Dog Handler — by Will B. Bitte

The Most Awesome Ginger Bastard In The Army — by O.Range

The Sexiest Bastard In The British Army — by F.Inledge

Don't Fuck With The British Army — by F. Inledges & R. Thybest

Some Other Titles To Give To Mates As A Wind Up
If you Can't Take A Joke you Shouldn't Have Joined

The Army's Worst Sniper — by Mr Gain

The Tightest Bastard In The British Army — by U.O Miakwid

The Laziest Bastard In The British Army — by I. Kipoften

The Most Awesome Spud Basher In The Army — by Edward King

The Biggest Slapper Shagger In The British Army — by Seph Philis & Gnr Rear

The Biggest Pad Shagger In The Army	by Noah Scrooples
The Ugliest Bastard In The British Army	by Neil Secks
The Army's Biggest Bed Wetter	by I.P Knightly
The Biggest Gaylord In The British Army	by Private Cockwatcher
The Army's Biggest Whinger	by Noah Moore-Tabin
The Grumpiest Bastard In The Army	by F.O Uprich
The Biggest Bullshitter In The Army	by Ely Moore
The Biggest Pisshead In The Army	by I. Lycabier
The Biggest Skiving Bastard In The Army	by I. Goh-Diffy
The Biggest Skiving Blanket Stacker In The Army	by I. Goh-Diffy
The Gobbiest Bastard In The Army	by Buster Gain
The Most Unfit Bastard In The British Army	by I.C Stickybuns
The Biggest Walking Sick Chit In The Army	by I. Milligane & Will B. Wurckshy
The Biggest Chin Strapped Knacker In The Army	by Don Keigh & Wayne Kerr
The Oldest Bastard In The Army	by Dai Nosaw
The Biggest Brown Nose In The Army	by R. Slicker

Veteran

The Most Awesome Army Veteran	by U.R.A Leg End
Grumpy Old Army Veteran	by Mo Knee
Don't Fuck With A Grumpy Old Army Veteran	by P. Stagain

Special Forces/Private Security

The Most Awesome Special Forces Operator	By Walt "Wally" Mitty & Ely Moore
The Biggest Bullshitter On The Circuit	By Walt "Wally" Mitty & Ely Moore
The Oldest Bastard On The Circuit	By S.L.R Fann

Search : Squaddie Brand Publishing on amazon by Regiment